PORTRAIT OF
HENLEY-ON-THAMES
BRITISH COUNTRY LANDSCAPES, TRADITIONS AND COMMUNITY LIFE

JIM DONAHUE

HALSGROVE

First published in Great Britain in 2015

British Library Cataloguing-in-Publication Data
A CIP record for this title is available from the British Library

ISBN 978 0 85704 263 7

HALSGROVE
Halsgrove House, Ryelands Business Park,
Bagley Road, Wellington, Somerset TA21 9PZ
Tel: 01823 653777   Fax: 01823 216796
email: sales@halsgrove.com

Part of the Halsgrove group of companies.
Information on all Halsgrove titles is
available at: www.halsgrove.com

Printed in China by the Everbest Printing Co Ltd

Contents

1. Introduction   5

2. The Henley Royal Regatta (HRR)   19

3. Henley Countryside Views   30
   - Spring   31
   - Summer   41
   - Autumn   51
   - Winter   61

4. Local Businesses   73

5. Community Groups   84

6. Competitive Sports   90

7. Traditions   105

8. Music and the Arts   127

Henley Town Hall overlooking Market Square.

1. Introduction

MOST PEOPLE KNOW of Henley from the annual Regatta that attracts competitors and visitors from around the world during the first week in July. Images of flamboyantly dressed people drinking Pimms at the exclusive Stewards Enclosure or a corporate hospitality marquee come to mind. Others may see it as an extremely well presented village on the Thames, home to various celebrities with impressive houses not accessible to your average homeowner.

With this book I attempt to capture the "real Henley", because there is so much more to it than these stereotypical images. It's true that people are proud to live here, but it's because the area has so much to offer. In 2014 *The Times* voted it the 12th best place to live in the countryside and 25th overall in 2015, while a survey by the *Telegraph* voted it among the 10 friendliest places to live, all of which I can clearly understand after spending more than a year getting to know its people and traditions.

I have used photography to try to convey the diversity of Henley life. While I will touch on its rich history, this is not meant to be a history book, but more a celebration of Henley life as it is today. You will also get to know some of its key traditions and residents, but it should also not be seen as catalogue of notable Henley institutions or people, as this short book can only scratch the surface. The book is more an attempt to capture the essence or spirit of the Henley area through photographs of its "Landscapes, Traditions, and Community Life".

To give it the coverage it deserves, this book covers the course of a year from about March 2014 to March 2015 to experience a full cycle of community events as well as the scenery throughout the four seasons.

The first records of Henley go back to the twelfth Century when it was apparently developed as a "planned medieval town" by royal initiative. Factors in this decision are likely to include the Roman road from Dorchester that goes through what is now the Fair Mile, as well as access to the river and agricultural abundance. By 1250 Henley was a flourishing market town, participating in river trade. By then a wooden bridge across the river was established.

A Henley Manor House on the site of today's Fawley Court and Phyllis Court Club, existed from the fourteenth century.

1540 – St Mary's iconic bell tower was built.

1690s – Flemish painter Jan Siberecht's paintings of Henley, including "View of Henley from Wargrave Road", (right) depicted agricultural trade on the river and a view of the old wooden bridge.

1738-1751 – Frederick, Price of Wales (father of George III) lived at Park Place, at Wargrave. It was sold to General Henry Seymour Conway who played a significant role in Henley's cultural and social life.

1771 – James Wyatt was commissioned to build Temple Island, by Sambrooke Freeman of Fawley Court. It was acquired by the Henley Royal Regatta (HRR) in 1987, which owns much of the meadows along the river.

1786 – Today's iconic five-arched bridge was built. A toll was required for almost100 years until the £10,000 debt was paid off. The heads of Thamesis (old Father Thames) and Isis, were designed by General Conway's daughter Mrs Anne Damer. They are thought to represent the joining of the Rivers Isis and Thame at Dorchester to form the Thames. The emblems of the HRR headquarters and Leander Club are appropriately displayed above them on the left.

1796 – Henley's first Town Hall was built on Market Square.

1839 – First Henley Regatta held.

1857 – Henley Branch rail line opened.

1901 – Today's modern Town Hall completed.

Henley had over 170 hanging baskets displayed in recent summers in its bid to win a gold medal in Britain in Bloom. As with 2012 and 2013, it won a gold medal in the regional competition in 2014, but was only able to earn a silver at nationals – you can bet they will try again in 2015! Other typical scenes around the river include a band at Mill Meadows on a summer weekend and views of the Angel Inn from the Henley Bridge.

Clockwise from top left, a winter view from Gravel Hill; views of the former Brakspear malting houses and brewery; and a view of Bell Street, one of Henley's oldest.

Henley experienced a bit of an economic downturn in the 1830s to '50s when the Great Western Railway was built to Bristol, bypassing Henley. In 1857 the branch line to Twyford was opened, paving the way for continued growth and the establishment of Henley as a desirable resort location. As you can see above, it is still vital to Henley's economy with regular trains into London in as little as forty-five minutes. Thomas Octavius Higgs started a printing business in Henley in 1877, moving to its present location on Reading Road in 1885. It secured a contract to print the *Henley & South Oxfordshire Standard* in 1892 and continues to share offices with the *Henley Standard* today.

Can you guess where these doors are located? See the map in the back of the book.

The Henley Town Council full council meeting at the Town Hall, opposite page. Henley has 16 councillors that appoint a mayor from the majority party. Most councillors are either from the Conservative Party or the independent Henley Residents Group (HRG). In recent years, the HRG has had the largest number of councillors, appointing the mayor. Every year a new mayor is sworn in at the Mayor Making ceremony at the Town Hall. This is shown top left, where the outgoing Mayor Stefan Gawrysiak is followed out of the room by incoming Mayor Martin Akehurst. When they return to the room, Martin will be wearing the mayoral garments as the new mayor. At the national level, Henley has long been a Conservative stronghold. Henley has been a Conservative "safe seat" since Major Valentine Fleming (Ian Fleming's father) became MP in 1910. Prior to current Henley MP John Howell, the previous two MPs from Henley have both been leading members of the Conservative party: Michael Heseltine, MP from 1974-2001, who served in the Cabinet under both Margaret Thatcher and John Major; and Boris Johnson, MP from 2001-2008, currently Mayor of London.

There can be no denying that rowing is at the heart of Henley. These majestic statues of Olympic Gold medallists Sir Steve Redgrave and Sir Matthew Pinsent at the River and Rowing Museum seem entirely appropriate. Steve lives locally and has been active in the Regatta as vice chairman for several years, taking over chairmanship of the Regatta in 2015. The River and Rowing Museum, opened in 1998, is definitely worth a visit, not only for its fascinating history of rowing in the UK, but also for an excellent overview of the history of the town of Henley itself.

2. The Henley Royal Regatta (HRR)

FIRST HELD IN 1839, partly as a result of the first Cambridge/Oxford boat challenge held in Henley about ten years earlier, the Regatta soon proved so successful that it was expanded from one day to two the next year. As the Regatta's popularity has grown it has further expanded and since 1986 is now five days. The regatta has been known as Henley Royal Regatta since 1851, when Prince Albert became the first royal patron. Since his death, every reigning monarch has agreed to be the patron.

The reasons for its success are partly due to the beautiful setting and straight stretch of the river that is so amenable to racing. Nestled at the base of the Chilterns at the intersection of Berkshire to the south, Oxfordshire to the north and Buckinghamshire to the northeast, it is what many consider to be the nicest stretch of the River Thames.

The course is marked out by two lines of booms (wooden bars which float on the water, secured between vertical poles), which are placed along the river to form a straight course about 1 mile and 550 yards (2112 metres), from the bottom of Temple Island upstream towards Henley Bridge (left). A crew from Eton prepares to start a race, above.

The course has been used for the Olympic rowing competitions when the Olympics were held in London in 1908 and 1948. In 2012 the Olympic rowing was held at the new man-made rowing lake at nearby Dorney.

Grace Kelly had a number of connections to the Regatta. Her father, Olympic champion John B. Kelly, had been controversially banned from Henley Regatta in the 1920s because he had worked as a bricklayer. This did not comply with the HRR strict rules on amateurism, but many saw it as an attempt to prevent an American from winning the Diamond Single Sculls Cup. The rules excluding manual labourers were later changed.

Grace Kelly attended several times, shown with her brother, Jack Kelly, Jr. who won the Diamonds Sculls in 1947 and in 1949. She dated Olympic champion Bert Bushnell and the 1950s' winner Tony Rowe before finding fame on the screen. Princess Grace of Monaco was the Regatta prize giver in 1981 and in 2003 the Women's Quadruple Sculls trophy was named in her memory.

A plaque on the floor of the Angel on the Bridge pub commemorates one of her visits.

The Regatta isn't only about the rowing, of course. Many spectators choose to watch up close from private pleasure craft, while others have access to the exclusive Stewards' Enclosure at the finish line, shown on the opposite page. Given the restricted numbers and waiting list, from which preference is given to those who have competed at the Regatta, it could take up to ten years before an applicant is likely to be elected to membership. The traditional dress code for the Stewards' Enclosure is strictly enforced. It states *"Gentlemen are required to wear lounge suits, or jackets or blazers with flannels, and a tie or cravat. Ladies are required to wear dresses or skirts with a hemline below the knee and will not be admitted wearing divided skirts, culottes or trousers of any kind. Similarly, no one will be admitted to the Stewards' Enclosure wearing shorts or jeans. Whilst not a requirement, it is customary for ladies to wear hats."* Mobile phones are also not allowed, but you can get away with it if you are discreet.

A picnic lunch is very much part of the Regatta tradition. Many of those with Stewards' Enclosure membership make use of their reserved parking space to have a picnic lunch by their car, some quite grand. Bristol University Rowing Alumni picnic in their stripy blazers, above. On the opposite page clockwise from top left, Tom Garnier, David Perry, and Jeremy Lewis enjoy a reunion. Tom Garnier has a connection back to the very start of the Regatta's history. His great-great-great grandfather rowed in the first Oxford-Cambridge boat race for Oxford in 1829 that led to the start the regatta ten years later; Dave Hull and Stuart Cheatle enjoy a beer at the Leander Club; students from Westminster College in London enjoy Pimm's along the Thames on the public stretch of the course; and Regatta Steward Adrian James.

But ultimately the Regatta is about the rowing competition. There are 20 events in total: six classes of race for Eights, five for Fours (three coxless and two coxed), five for Quadruple Sculls, and races for Coxless Pairs and Double Sculls. In addition there are single sculling races for both men and women. 1993 was the first year women competed when a new event for Women Single Scullers was inaugurated. Every year Henley is visited by many crews from abroad and in 2013 86 crews were from overseas. Given the limited number of hotels in the area, the Henley community pitches in. Henley "landladies" have traditionally offered accommodation at their family homes to visiting foreign crews. They will typically need to accommodate 10 people as a crew of 8 plus their coach and cox all prefer to stay together. On the opposite page, Pangbourne College crew prepare for their race in front of the royal barge *Gloriana*, and a Canadian crew, above, make an extra effort at the finishing line.

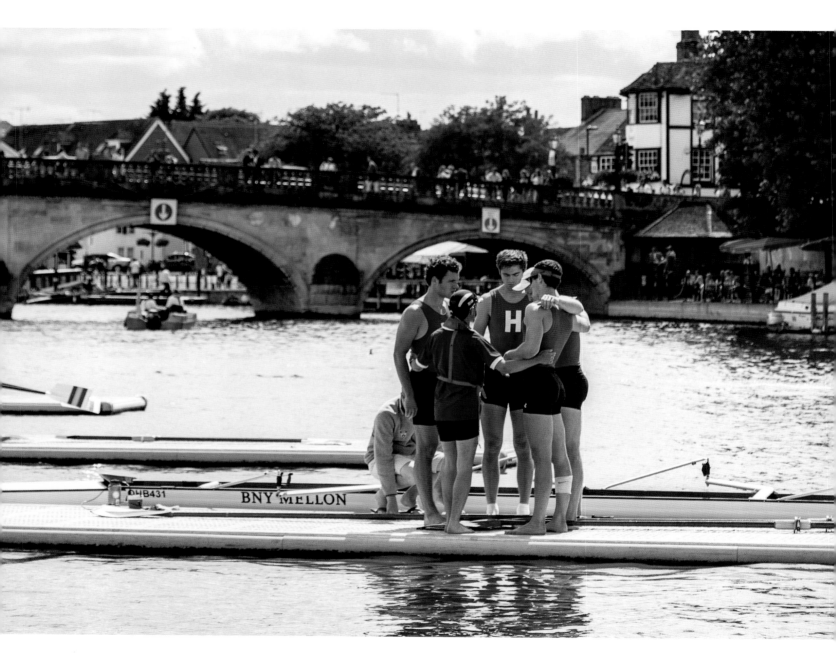

A win at Henley Regatta is the ultimate triumph for most rowers. The Newcastle University team celebrate their win over Harvard in the Prince Albert Challenge Cup, above. The race was originally known as the Men's Student Coxed Fours. The Harvard team console each other after their loss, opposite page. In 2010, the Regatta featured in the Hollywood film *The Social Network*, in which Leander Club rowers recreated a 2004 race that included the Winklevoss twins, rivals of Facebook founder Mark Zuckerburg from Harvard. As with the lawsuit against Facebook, the Winklevoss twins and the Harvard University team were unable to prevail against their Dutch rivals to win The Grand Challenge Cup.

3. Henley Countryside Views

ONE OF THE GREAT pleasures of living in the Henley area is the scenery of the surrounding countryside and the villages that make up the larger Henley community. Henley is nestled between the south edge of the Chilterns, with the hills rising just behind the Town Hall up Gravel Hill, and the Berkshire Downs rising above the Thames and Remenham Hill to the south. Because of the exceptional beauty, I have dedicated one of the larger chapters of this book to the scenery and landscape views of the area throughout the four seasons. The locations of many of these landscapes can be seen in a map at the back of the book to help you explore them for yourself.

SPRING

The Henley area has some of England's finest bluebell woods, such as these at Park Corner, below. On the opposite page, bright yellow rapeseed can be seen in April in many areas, including this view of Fawley Court to the north, as seen across the Thames from Remenham Hill. Fawley Court was one of the original manor houses of Henley until it was sold to Sir James Whitelocke in 1616. In 1684, the house was completely rebuilt for William Freeman in its present red brick state. It sits along the Regatta course, and is an approximate mid-way landmark for the rowers.

Above, you can see the ancient Wittenham Clumps in the distance from Ewelme House near Crocker End. Once the site of Iron Age forts, they have a mystical air about them. Further spring scenes around the Henley area are shown on the opposite page.

Hambleden church at a spring sunset on the opposite page and the former WH Smith House, above. Hambleden and the surrounding valley is a magical place and a quintessentially English village unchanged over the centuries. So much so that there have been no shortage of films and TV shows shot in the area, including Tim Burton's 1999 version of *Sleepy Hollow*, and scenes from *Nanny McPhee*, *101 Dalmatians*, HBO's *Band of Brothers*, and 2015's *Into the Woods*. In the early 1870s the Estate was acquired by The Rt Hon W H Smith MP, later the 1st Viscount Hambleden, whose father founded the famous firm of newsagents. In 2008, the village, including 44 houses, a pub, and 1600 acres of forest and countryside was controversially sold to Swiss financier Urs Schwarzenbach, although even this doesn't seem to have changed anything about this timeless place.

On the left, a seasonal wading stream that sometimes flows through Skirmett in the spring. Above, another view of rapeseed field in April from near Down Farm by Ewelme.

View near Marsh Lock, left, and horses grazing by the Round House Farm at Fawley, below. On the opposite page, signs of spring life include, clockwise from top left, hazel catkins, sycamore buds, daffodils, horse chestnut buds and fully sprouted, and cherry blossom buds in front of Remenham church.

SUMMER

Summer is of course the time to make the most of the great outdoors in Britain. It is when the festivals such as the Regatta, Henley Festival, Rewind and Henley Show all take place. The spring grass starts to turn brown and the evenings are long, often not getting dark until 10pm in June. On the opposite page, the summer harvest hay bales can be seen with grazing cows in the distance near the road to Hurley. An evening view of rolling Chiltern Hills at Stonor is shown above. On the following pages is one of my favourite views over Bix Bottom Farm on a misty June morning.

Above, view towards the Hambleden valley from the woods above the Henley Showgrounds. On the opposite page, clockwise from top left: Mountain bikers Paul Steiger and Carey Sayer making the most of the summer weather. The Frog at Skirmett is a pub and restaurant recommended if just to enjoy its idyllic location in the Hambleden valley. The windmill overlooking the nearby village of Turville was used as the home of Caractacus Potts in the 1969 movie *Chitty Chitty Bang Bang*, based on the book by local author Ian Fleming. The picturesque village of Turville was also the setting for the popular *Vicar of Dibley* TV series.

Harvest View over the Stonor Valley.

Above, rowers making the most of a lovely summer's evening, approach Henley from upstream. Other summer scenes on the opposite page include some misty morning views of swans and cygnets on the Thames near Hambleden Lock, typical of late August or September.

AUTUMN

Autumn means an end to summer holidays and increasingly longer nights, but it is many people's favourite time of year due to the crisper weather and constantly changing views and smells it brings. An impressive avenue of lime trees at Burrow Farm near Rotten Row at Hambleden, opposite. The Burrow Farm gardens are normally open to visitors two Sundays in June and July every year. Mountain biking amongst the golden beech woods near Nettlebed, above.

An autumn view near Greys Court, above. On the opposite page, autumn scenes include fallen acorns and oak leaves, multi-coloured beech leaves and nuts, alder catkins and cones, and an example of the hundreds of varieties of mushrooms that can be found in the local woods.

Above, sheep enjoying a beautiful autumn day and a fine view of Hambleden village. On the opposite page, clockwise from top left: horse chestnut tree about to bear its seed, known by school children as conkers; a couple enjoying the Guy Fawkes bonfire celebration by the Henley Rugby Club; the Henley entrance along the Fair Mile; an abundance of blackberries can be found along bramble hedgerows.

A pair of rowers, as seen though the mist early on an autumn morning. This photo was taken from near the Hambleden Lock in the grounds of the Henley Business School which is shown on the opposite page, top. The building, known as Greenlands, was previously owned by William Henry Smith, son of the founder of W H Smith before the family moved to Hambleden. The house received a cool reception from Jerome K. Jerome who joked in *Three Men in a Boat* that it was "the rather uninteresting-looking river residence of my newsagent." The old Mill House at Hambleden Lock, is shown on the bottom, left.

Left: The Maharaja's Well in Stoke Row, on the left, is an unusual and exotic feature for an English country village. It was built in 1863 by the Maharajah of Benares, along with a cherry orchard to provide for the well's upkeep. The Maharaja wanted to repay a debt for the work that a local squire from Ipsden, Edward Reade, had done in building a well in India previously. While in India, Mr Reade had told the Maharaja of water deprivation in his home area of Ipsden.

Above: Large herds of fallow deer can be seen throughout the woods, such as these near Stoke Row, sometimes in numbers greater than 100.

Stoke Row and the surrounding area was also quite active in the World War Two war effort. Stoke Row became a top supplier of wooden tent pegs, reportedly producing over 3 million pegs. The woods around Highmoor and Nettlebed were also used to gather a large contingent of US forces, including tanks and other vehicles prior to the D-Day invasion in 1944. Signs of the paved roads from this can still be found in the woods.

The Black Horse Pub in Checkendon is an example of a traditional country pub that is still as it was a century ago. It is tucked away in a quiet woodland setting, so you may need to ask a local for directions! Owners Margaret and Martin Morgan are shown above. They both live in the pub with their children who also work at the pub. Margaret was born in the pub that her family first bought in 1905. A Black Horse regular enjoys a traditional ale, above right.

After the Second World War, a Polish resettlement camp was based in Checkenden not far from where the where the Black Horse pub is today. The camp was built to support displaced Polish families resulting from Nazi and Stalinist invasions in 1940, and many chose to stay after the war settlement divided Poland's territory, and what was left became a communist 'puppet state' of the Soviets. Martin Morgan of the Black Horse remembers riding his bicycle to the camp with his friends as teens. Sometimes he would go there to watch English films which were shown in the theatre / cinema building. The camp closed in 1961, but remains can still be seen in the nearby woods, right.

WINTER

The views around Henley can be just as varied and impressive in the winter, although you have to take advantage of the good weather when you get it. It can also be wet, as shown on the following pages, and the days are particularly short in December, when it starts getting dark as early as 3:30pm. Although snow is not common, it often goes below freezing and the resulting frost adds to the beauty of the countryside such as in the pictures on these pages. Farmers up early at Mill End Farm near Hambleden Lock above, and chimney smoke rises near Bix Bottom, opposite.

January and February of 2014 resulted in record rains and the river extended well into the flood plains resulting in damage and disruption. An indication of the flooding is shown with the 'Ama of the Thames' mermaid statue outside the Red Lion Hotel. The statue is normally on a patio used for serving meals at the Red Lion Hotel, but she seemed happy to join the river again. The cricket field, above, as well as most of the Regatta site was also well under water, but magically recovered in time for summertime activities. On the following pages, a frosty sunrise by the Thames near the Henley Business School.

A view across Hambleden Common on a frosty January morning, above. On the opposite page, clockwise from top left, a wintry sunset behind barren trees, some frosty rose hips, snowdrops, and a sign for the ancient Ridgeway trail that passes through Swyncombe. Snowdrops come out as early as January as one of the first sign of spring life. Swyncombe's St Botolph's church has a particular abundance of snowdrops and holds a Snowdrop Festival every February, that includes a blessing from the Vicar and tea and cakes for all.

Frosty and hazy view over Skirmett and the Hambleden valley.

View from Ewelme church and almshouses at sunset above. The church is part of an even more picturesque village and well worth a visit. Jerome K Jerome, author of *Three Men in a Boat* is buried in the graveyard. The church was used to film scenes from 2012's *Les Miserables*. Opposite page, clockwise from top left: a winter walk with a view of Thames near Mapledurham; reintroduced to the area in 1997, red kites are now plentiful and a common sight; swans at Henley with the Leander Club in the background; view over the Thames towards Wargrave and the grounds of Park Place and Conway's Bridge. The bridge is a rustic arched stone structure on the estate of Park Place that still carries traffic on the Wargrave road. It was designed by Humphrey Gainsborough, brother of the artist Thomas Gainsborough, and built in 1763. Park Place, as noted earlier, was previously the residence of Frederick, Prince of Wales, and then General Conway. In 2011 it was sold to a Russian financier and businessman for £140 million making it the most expensive house ever sold in the UK.

4. Local Businesses

LORRAINE HILLER, seated left, has been running her 1950s' style Hot Gossip Coffee shop on Friday Street since 2007. As a civic-minded town councillor since 1999, she has been keen to encourage its use as a meeting place for youth and other community groups. In 2013 she expanded into teas with Upstairs & Downstairs on Duke Street. It offers a loose-leaf tea emporium downstairs, and a traditional tearoom upstairs, complete with art deco china, white linen, and cakes made with 1930s' recipes, shown left. Florist Annette March shows off her Christmas themed display at White GDN flower shop on Hart Street, above.

Clockwise from top left, if you need a pair of reasonably priced glasses or watch band repair, Brian Poole is the man to see at his stall by the Waitrose car park; Laurence Morris of Laurence Menswear in Duke Street, fitting a jacket for Patrick Collins; Hillary Redhead of the Bell Bookshop shows off one her favourite books of the year, *Mrs. Hemingway*; and Oxfam Book & Music shop manager Sabine Adams, displays a signed copy of a book by the recently deceased John Mortimer, who was a Henley regular, living in the Hambleden valley.

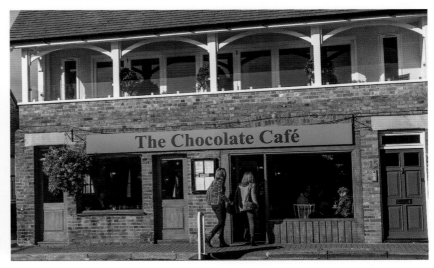

Diana Cook of Way's Rare and Secondhand Books in Friday Street, top. Diane has been running Way's with her partner Richard Way since 1976 and seems to know all there is to know about books. And they don't just sell rare books, but offer a wide range of low cost second-hand books – so go in and explore! Below, Vivienne Lee of the Chocolate Café. Just opposite the river by the bridge, it is one of the nicest locations in Henley to meet for coffee or breakfast. It gets its name from the chocolates, cakes, and pastries that her business partner Roy Hastings specialises in.

Above: Rob Griffiths and Lawrence Plant run Athletes Service at their impressive facilities at the old Oast House at Greys Road Car Park. It includes a triathlon-focussed shop, an endless swimming pool, a full gym, numerous treatment rooms, and an espresso bar. Both former rowers, they offer pilates and yoga classes as well as access to a variety of therapists specialising in sports injury treatment and prevention.

Top left: TV Celebrity Chef Antony Worral Thompson, runs the Greyhound Pub and restaurant in Rotherfied Peppard that features seasonal food supporting local producers, with live music every Wednesday.

Left: Gillian Nahum of the Boatique shop on Friday Street offers a nautical themed emporium ranging from clothing to gifts. She also runs Henley Boat Sales and Charters specialising in classic boats.

YEUK is a skateboard shop founded in Henley in 2012 by Steve Terry, shown above with James Lipscombe. YEUK now boasts its own branded range of Skateboard clothing, a popular on-line shop, and a second branch in Marlow. Along with Colin Brathwaite, they are leading a Henley Skateboard Park Initiative to replace the existing aging park. Together, they convinced the Town Council of the need for this and are now moving ahead with plans to build it in the near future.

Clockwise from top left: St Audrey's Gift & Art Market has been on Duke Street since 2010 offering an eclectic mix of gifts, prints, and greetings cards; Gabriel Machin Butchers has been an institution in Henley sine 1910 and Ian Blanford has run the shop since 2002; Henley Nails and Brows beauty salon in Duke Street was opened in 2011 by former Henley College student Cassy Richardson; Amy McNally and Kirsty Chapman at the Lemongrove Gallery which has been in Duke Street since 2007.

Stuart Turner, above, has been manufacturing motorised engines and water pumps in Henley since 1906. Along with Invesco Perpetual, which is one of the UK's largest independent investment fund managers, Stuart Turner remains one of Henley's largest employers.

Angie Best's Metaphysical Gym offers first class training facilities and staff, with a picturesque view of the Thames, by the Henley Business School off the Marlow Road. Angie, previously married to footballer George Best, has spent most of her adult life as a physical fitness trainer. Angie is shown, right, during a personal training session with Briony Geekie, local Henley chiropractor.

This page: After being brewed in Henley for over 200 years, Brakspear closed its Henley brewery operations in 2002, choosing to outsource the brewing to Marston's Wychwood Brewery near Oxford under license agreement. Brakspear's Head Office is still in Henley by the Bull in Bell Street where a limited amount of Brakspear specialty beer is brewed, normally changed monthly. Brakspear CEO Tom Davies is shown sampling Old Ale, which was brewed at the original Henley Brewery. Brakspear still owns 11 pubs in Henley and 75 more within a 10-mile radius.

Opposite: Jeff Rosenmeir moved to Henley in 1996 and started selling locally-brewed Lovibonds beer in 2005. He brews the beer at the Chiltern Valley Winery & Brewery near Hambleden, and runs a packaging facility, shop and tasting room in Henley town centre behind Market Place in a historic building that was once home to a John Lovibonds and Sons depot and shop, long since closed, hence the name. Originally from Wisconsin in the US, he brews a number of varieties including an increasingly popular Americanised version of British IPA called 69 IPA that is "colder, fizzier and hoppier tasting" than traditional British ales.

The Bird in Hand pub in Greys Road, above, won the award for best pub in South Oxfordshire by the Campaign for Real Ale in 2014 for the fourth time. Landlord Graham Steward, shown above right, says, "We are a friendly local pub. Everybody knows everybody and we always make people feel welcome to have a chat."

The Bird in Hand is also home to a monthly music quiz run by Andy Tucker, right, of Henley's In The Groove Record Shop. The quiz night is usually a full house with music aficionados of all ages, opposite page. On the night I attended the main topic of the quiz was related to the band The Who. In The Groove Records specialises in used vinyl records, as well as used CDs and DVDs.

5. Community Groups

AT HIS INAUGURAL address, incoming Mayor Martin Akehurst marvelled at the community spirit of Henley, recalling that they had recently tried to count the number of community groups in Henley, and they got up to over 200, and were still counting. Not all are charitable or civic minded, some are more hobbies or clubs, but there is certainly no reason not to get involved in Henley.

Andrew Hawkins has had the same Allotment plot at Greencroft, by the Cricket Field, for over thirty years and has been Chairman of the Allotments Association for twenty. He says the '10 pole' size of allotments was originated in the nineteenth century by landowners to give low paid workers enough land to feed their family but not so much to allow them to sell for a profit or to make them too tired to be productive workers.

The *Henley Standard* lists 15 local Women's Institute (WI) branches. Originally started during the First World War to give women an opportunity to support each other while men were off at war, it now has more than 6,500 branches in the UK and is one of the largest campaigning groups for women. A typical meeting will include a speaker and lots of tea, cake, and biscuits. The Grey's WI meeting above featured a harvest theme with a demonstration about the tradition of making corn dollies.

The Henley Choral Society at rehearsal for its annual Christmas Concert at St Mary's church, above. Formed in 1973, they are led by conductor Benjamin Goodson, having weekly practices and normally performing three concerts a year. No auditions are required, but they aim for the highest singing standards. Benjamin has also recently introduced youth choirs.

Clockwise from top left: The Henley Symphony Orchestra at their Christmas concert. Formed in 1970, they are led by conductor Ian Brown. Like the Choral Society, they rehearse weekly for normally three concerts a year.

The Henley in Transition sustainability group drum up support for the National Climate March to be held in London in March, outside the Town Hall.

The 1st Henley Brownies troop at Harpsden Village Hall, left, learning the deaf alphabet, working towards their Disability Awareness badge. The girls are led by Michaela Clarke, who also works to keep the community well informed through her Henley Herald on-line newspaper.

It's a relatively well-kept secret that the mountain biking in the Henley area is amongst the best in the country if not the world. Spoilt for choice of endless miles of bridle paths with the Chiltern Hills offering just the right level of challenging climbs and descents – as long as you don't mind a little mud from time to time.

A discussion group called the Sceptics and Believers was formed at a local pub by religious sceptic Ed Atkinson and Christian Mark Wójcicki. The group is open to anyone and is shown here at their new larger venue at the Rugby Club, during a talk about the meaning of life by theologian and author Os Guinness. Ed says of the group "We value the chance to meet and discuss our deeply held views on life and meaning in a friendly setting where we have freedom to speak without fear of causing offence."

An elaborate Murder Mystery evening, complete with scripted actors and an audience, held at Hardwick House at nearby Whitchurch on Thames, by Henley's Tug Boat Book Club, led by Harriet Wynn-Jones. The Murder Mystery is one of many social events put on by the club, this being in honour of member Maggie Atkinson's birthday, standing, above far right. Hardwick House and Estate is home to the Rose family and was home to Sir Charles Day Rose (1847 - 1913), whose interests included horseracing, motorcars, yachting, and aviation, and is said to have been one of the models for "Toad of Toad Hall" in Kenneth Graeme's *Wind in the Willows*. Grahame's illustrator E. H. Shepherd is said to have used parts of Hardwick House in his drawings.

6. Competitive Sports

THE COMPETITIVE SPIRIT of the Regatta seems to have rubbed off on the other sporting activities so that Henley boasts more world class sporting teams and events than many much larger towns. The GS Henley (Gruppo Sportivo) road cycling club, normally has about four different groups riding on Saturday mornings from Starbucks, grouped by the average speed of the riders. On the opposite page, clockwise from top left: The Henley Red Kites football team, against visiting Brackley Town; Henley Hockey player Mae Reineke, age forteen, on the Ladies Team 2, one of 11 Henley teams; Dragon boat racing may not seem overly competitive, but don't try telling that to the Henley Dragons racing team; the Henley Classic Swim follows the 2.1km Henley Royal Regatta course upstream, very early on the Sunday morning before the Wednesday start of the Regatta. The swim started in 2004 when two former rowers Tom Kean and Jeremy Laming decided to swim the regatta course without permission at dawn. It now includes 85 swimmers from around the world every year, some competitive, others just doing it for the experience.

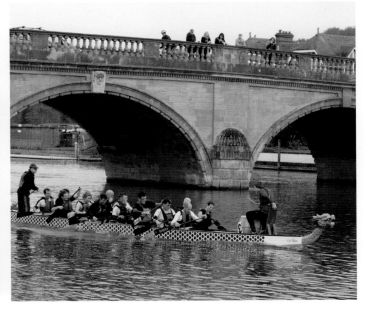

Henley Hawks' flanker Tom Hall making a break in a match against the Cornish All Blacks from Launceston, above. To his right, looking cheerful at his prospects is Henley's leading scorer, fly-half James Comben. In a tight match, the Hawks prevailed by 1 point. The men's Henley Hawks team was relegated to National Division 2 in the spring of 2014, but are now strong leaders of Division 2 as of 2015. Henley has about 20 different rugby teams, including seven for "minis" ranging from Under 6 to Under 12 years of age, five teams for ages 13-16, two "colts" teams for 17-18 year olds, and six "senior" teams including the women's Hawks who were promoted to National Division 1 in 2014.

For many Henley residents, just the view of the Henley cricket team playing at the Brakspear grounds from the road leading up Remenham Hill is satisfaction enough. But the competitive Henley team has now won the Home Counties Premier League championship in both 2013 and 2014. The Henley team is only one of many local teams as every self-respecting village must sport their own cricket pitch and team, including Hambleden, Stonor, Crazies Hill, Cockpole Green, Stoke Row, Harpsden, Whitchurch, Turville, Ewelme, Stonor, Nettlebed, and Greys Green shown above at a tea break.

Greys Green cricket pitch, above, on a perfect summer's day. On the opposite page, more views of Henley and Greys Green cricket.

The Leander Club, above, located on the Berkshire side of the river immediately next to the Henley Bridge, is home to the UK's leading rowers. The club is home to both junior (15-18s) and senior men's and women's teams. Team GB rowers are also based at the Leander Club. Team GB Head Coach Jürgen Grobler, opposite top left, lives in Henley. He led GB teams to gold medals from 1992 - 2012, including Steve Redgrave and Matthew Pinsent. Since 1908, the club has won 112 Olympic and Paralympic medals, which some may argue makes it the most successful sporting club in the world. Leander Club Chief Coach Mark Banks, who also lives in Henley, is shown giving advice, below right. Always big winners at the Henley Regatta, in 2014 the club qualified for 14 events with 58 athletes, 18 of them Team GB members, and won 6 cups.

Besides the world class Leander Club, the Henley Rowing Club and the Upper Thames Rowing Club (UTRC) are the two main rowing clubs in Henley for those not able to pursue rowing as a full time profession. The Henley Rowing Club has a large and well-medalled junior women's rowing team, shown above. On the opposite page top left, Henley coach David Lister is shown in the red jacket coaching by bicycle. Three crews from the Henley Rowing Club took home trophies at the 2014 Henley Women's Regatta held in June. Founded in 1839, about the same time as the Henley Regatta, the Henley Rowing club won its first Henley Regatta cup in 2005. The Upper Thames Rowing Club, only fifty years old, were thrilled to win their first cups at Henley in 2014.

Cambridge women console each other after loss to Oxford in Henley Boat Races held in March, which include lightweight crew races and the women's equivalent to the men's heavyweight Boat Race held in London at Putney. The women's race is due to move to the London course in 2015 equivalent to the men's. The Henley Boat Races are one of many rowing events and "Heads" put on by the local clubs in addition to the HRR during the rowing season. You may not think of chess, table tennis, and billiards as competitive sports, but there are local leagues in each of these events that include Henley teams. The same of course goes for show horse competitions. Fourteen-year-old Clare Higgins from Stoke Row is shown with her horse at one of the many equestrian competitions held at the Henley Showground each year.

7. Traditions

SOME THINGS HAVEN'T changed much over the years, as the traditional activities in this section demonstrate. You may also notice that, in most cases, people like to dress in traditional clothing appropriate for the occasion. The pheasant shooting season runs from October 1st to February 1st. On these pages and the following two I feature photos from two shoots, one held at Lord Phillimore's estate at Binfield Heath not far from the family home at Coppid Hall in Shiplake, and one held at Swyncombe (above, opposite), organised by local resident Stephen Christie-Miller who also runs the Henley Branch of Savill's Estate Agents. As with many traditions, the social aspects of the events are as important as the actual shooting.

It is well known that Fox Hunting has been illegal in the UK since 2005. However the tradition lives on in the form of trail hunting, where organisers lay scents at various locations for the hounds to hunt instead of live animals. Organised hunts such as the Kimblewick Hunt shown here at Whitchurch are still common.

The Symm International Horse trials held at Hambleden in April include three days of competition that include Dressage, Show Jumping, and the Cross Country Steeplechase, shown left. 2014's competitors included Zara Phillips, member of the Great Britain Olympic Team and the Queen's granddaughter.

The Henley Show is a traditional agricultural show held on the second Saturday of September. It is held at Greenland Farm in Hambleden and in recent years has attracted over 17,000 visitors. As you can see from the photos it includes all types of competitions and demonstrations – everything from sheep shearing to horse-drawn carriages, and a great day out!

The ploughing match at Dunsden is seen as an offshoot of the Henley Show and is normally held a few weeks later in early October. For those not familiar with a ploughing match, the objectives seem to be related to the "straightness, uniformity, and firmness" of the furrows, amongst other factors. On the opposite page, top right, Katie Pentecost treats Moonbeam the ferret to frozen custard. The many local activities that Lady Judy and Sir William McAlpine of Fawley, bottom right, are involved in include being patrons of the Agriculture Society and former presidents of the Henley Show. Dave Craig uses a tape measure to ensure ploughing accuracy.

The Greys Green Summer Fête held at historic Greys Court is one of many local village fêtes held every summer. For many it's an opportunity to support the community and catch up with neighbours. One not so traditional activity includes Giorgia Fiorentino trying the Wellie Throw, above. On the opposite page, clockwise from top left: the Goring and Streatley Concert Band; former Henley Mayor Stefan Gawrysiak runs the tombola raffle with partner Catherine; Matt and Leanne Ellard selling cakes and biscuits; and Amanda Gibbon and Elizabeth Hodgkins, also a former Henley Mayor, supervising the Wombles fly wire game, watched by Sophie Hughes, right.

Croquet, boating, and bridge are among of the traditions practiced at Phyllis Court Club. Situated along the Thames just opposite the Stewards' Enclosure at the Regatta finish line, it is an ideal place to enjoy Regatta Week festivities in an exclusive setting. The club was formed in 1905, but the history goes back much further. A building at this site was the manor house of Henley since the 1300s, then known as Fillets Court. It later became part of neighbouring Fawley Court Manor. While it is still a popular private club and Henley institution, times have changed since its heyday in the first half of the twentieth century when there were frequent visits from royalty and foreign dignitaries and membership included large numbers of landed gentry and titled aristocrats.

The Remembrance Sunday ceremonies in November took on new significance in 2014 with the 100th Anniversary of the start of the First World War. Led by the Chaplain of St Mary's outside the Town Hall, the service includes the Mayor, the full Town Council, the Henley MP, members of the Royal British Legion, the Territorial Army and several other leading Henley organisations all dressed in full uniform to pay tribute to those who gave their lives for the country. At the conclusion of the ceremony each organisation takes it in turn to lay a wreath of poppies at the War Memorial at the base of the Town Hall which this year included wreaths from the brownies and the Henley 'minis' rugby team, amongst many others.

The streets of Henley town centre are all closed for the annual Christmas Festival in early December that marks the official start of the Christmas season. The Mayor and Town Crier light the Christmas tree, the shops are open late, the streets are filled with stalls and amusement park rides, and it is probably the busiest night of the year for the pubs.

The Christmas festival is particularly popular with the younger crowd, although it is a festive night for the whole town. There is also no shortage of sausages, including those cooked by Antony Worrall Thompson outside Gabriel Machins Butchers, bottom right.

But Christmas in Henley doesn't stop there. Henley was one of the first towns to offer a Living Advent Calendar, where the community is treated to different entertainment for 24 nights, each at different venues across town. Clockwise from top left, a duo singing "Baby its Cold Outside"; Rupert House School girls singing carols; the 'No Directions' band cover of David Bowie's *Major Tom*; cabaret-style singer Baroness Maria von Hackemann at Phyllis Court.

And no Christmas would be complete without a visit to the Christmas Tree Barn at Christmas Common, top row. While the name of Christmas Common village pre-dates the Christmas tree farm by a few hundred years, Andrew Ingram, above right, has been growing Christmas trees there since 1971 with his wife Jane, with the business really taking off in the '80s and '90s. In 2011 and 2013 they won competitions to provide the 10 Downing Street Christmas tree and met Prime Minister David Cameron.

8. Music and the Arts

AS IN OTHER AREAS, Henley hits above its weight in cultural activities on offer, with what seems to be a growing number of festivals that include its own Fringe Festival, Literary Festival, Youth Festival, and Blues and Jazz Festival. The five-day black tie Henley Festival is probably the pinnacle, taking place the week after the Henley Regatta in July, using the grounds and grandstands from the Regatta along the river. If you've never been, I can only recommend it as a unique and magical experience. It features an array of art exhibitions, dining options, roving performance artists, such as those shown on the left, and big name music artists, that in 2014 included, Brian Ferry, Burt Bacharach, Joss Stone and the Jacksons, and the 2015 headliner is Lionel Richie. The following two pages offer a glimpse of the fun.

First started in 2009 by Henley resident David Heartfield, Rewind has become an annual tradition and the world's largest '80s festival, now with sister events in Scotland and Cheshire. Held in August from a Friday to Sunday, it attracts many visitors to the town, often camping on-site or at nearby camp grounds. Hobbs of Henley offers frequent water taxis between the town centre and the site at Temple Island Meadows at Remenham. The 2014 line-up included Bob Geldof's Boom Town Rats, UB40, Mike and the Mechanics, and Bonnie Tyler. The 2015 line-up includes OMD, Billy Ocean, and the Human League.

The Kenton Theatre was established in 1805, originally called the New Theatre as it was in New Street, making it the fourth oldest working theatre in the country. The theatre has had its ups and downs over the years, but it achieved a significant milestone in August 2010, when it was able to buy the freehold through fundraising in the Henley community, securing its viability as a theatre for the future. The Kenton supports a broad range of entertainment; sometimes running theatre shows prior to release in London's West End, musical acts such as Kiki Dee, shown right, and the recent *Peter Pan* Christmas pantomime.

The Henley Literary Festival, first started in 2006, has gone from strength to strength, establishing itself as one of Britain's leading literary festivals. Held at the end of September, it has been able to attract big names such as Melvyn Bragg and Kate Adie as well as those with local connections including Jeremy Paxman, Mike Read, Boris Johnson, and Steve Redgrave. With over 100 speakers to choose from, one of the great things about it is the chance to see your favourite authors at unique locations around town such as the popular "River Readings" that are performed while on a cruise down the Thames, shown left. Above left, local photographer Scarlet Page talks to BBC Radio 6 Music DJ Shaun Keaveney about her exhibition of photos of famous rock guitarists, including the one of her famous father behind them. A tribute to the fiftieth anniversary of *Chitty Chitty Bang Bang*, above, took place at the Kenton Theatre, with the original illustrator John Burningham, and readings by actor Simon Williams, best known for his role in *Upstairs Downstairs*.

James Bond and *Chitty Chitty Bang Bang* author, Ian Fleming, has many connections to Henley. As mentioned earlier, his father Major Valentine Fleming was MP for Henley from 1910 until his death in the First World War in 1917. The Sue Ryder Hospice in Nettlebed (above), known as Joyce Grove, was originally built in 1908 for Ian Fleming's great-grandfather, Scottish financier Robert Fleming. Ian Fleming's two nieces, Lucy and Kate Fleming, still live in the area, and are both active in the community including supporting the Kenton Theatre. Lucy is an actress and married to actor Simon Williams shown on the previous page at the Literary Festival. The statue above left was featured in the James Bond film *Goldeneye* and is sited on the estate near Nettlebed. It is made of fibreglass and was a gift to the Fleming family. It featured in the tank chase sequence but sadly the wings are no longer attached due to high winds.

Local teenagers are given a place to 'chill out' at Magoo's bar once a week to listen to and play music with access to mentors such as professional music agent, JJ, shown above centre. Georgi Michael, above left, is given the chance to perform informally at Acoustic@Magoos with a goal of preparing performances for the local Music on the Meadows youth music festival.

A recent addition to the summer music festival scene is the Hideaway Festival, left, so called because of its location in a beautifully hidden valley at Fawley in the grounds of Sir William McApline's Fawley estate. The 2014 festival featured local groups as well as bands like Alabama 3, Dreadzone, and Eddie and the Hot Rods.

In addition to the big festivals, top quality live music can be seen at a number of venues in the area. The Nettlebed Folk Club is regarded by many leading folk acts as one of the UK's top folk clubs. And you can enjoy live music nearly every Monday night, which normally includes a mixture of visiting folk artists and local resident musicians such the father and daughter duo "Kith and Kin", shown above.

The Crooked Billet in Stoke Row offers live music with a first class meal in an intimate, rural setting. Run by Chef Paul Clerehugh since 1989, above left, it is regarded as one the best restaurants in the area and even the UK. Paul can also be seen serving food at many Henley festivals and writes a regular food column for the Henley Standard. On music nights, you can see a wide range of well-known acts, such as Chris Jagger, brother of Sir Mick, who is described as a "rootsy bluesy acoustic foot stomper." It was also an old stomping ground of former Beatle George Harrison, who once performed there at a birthday party with guitar legend Gary Moore.

Photo by *Henley Standard*

Photo by Nick Hughes

Is Henley becoming Hollywood on Thames? As noted earlier, Hambleden is regularly used as a filming location including the 2014 film *Into the Woods*, shown above, where Johnny Depp was spotted by locals while here to shoot his role as the Wolf. Not that this is unusual for Henley. Locals are used to hearing that George Clooney, now living in nearby Sonning, has a new favourite Italian restaurant in Henley, or that Orlando Bloom, who has a home outside Henley, was seen the other day in Waitrose, or people commenting on the impressive size of the house Rowan Atkinson is building at Ipsden. Above left, Watlington resident Jeremy Irons is shown at an open gardens event at his home with members of the local Horticultural Society.

And there is a Midsomer Murders trail you can take that starts at Henley and goes through many villages in the surrounding area. The trail includes the Argyll Pub in Market Place, left, that now sells a special Midsomer Ale to celebrate the episodes it appeared in. Landlord Neil Ainsworth is shown with daughter Fran and local patron Nigel Barklem. The Nettlebed Folk club, shown on the previous page, has apparently featured in eight episodes and has even produced a special CD of folk music for the TV show.

Brad Pitt on the set of *Fury*, which was filmed on a farm near Watlington for seven weeks in the summer of 2013. Films like this support local businesses such as the Hotel du Vin and the LA Fitness health club said to be used by some of the crew. For 2014's *Imitation Game*, the Sue Ryder Hospice, shown on page 135, doubled as Bletchley Park. Actor Benedict Cumberbatch took time to visit patients at the Hospice during the filming. PHOTO BY GRAHAM STONE

Friar Park on Gravel Road was built in "spectacular eclectic style" by solicitor Frank Crisp around 1890, but it is best known as the home of Beatle's George Harrison from the early 1970's until his death in 2001. He built a state of the art recording studio there called FPSHOT (Friar Park Studio Henley on Thames) where most of his solo work was recorded. Michael Palin described visiting Geoerge in his diaries in the '70s and George taking him out to his local pub, the Row Barge in West Street, left. There are also stories of George performing at the pub with Eric Clapton. In the 1980s, despite increased security following John Lennon's death, he even took to the streets over redevelopment of the old Regal Cinema by a Waitrose. There have been talks of local memorials or annual concerts to celebrate his life, but currently all that remains is Friar Park and a tribute to one of his songs on the wall at the local Zizzi's restuarant.

Another important local rock history landmark is Hook End Manor at Checkendon. The original studio, Space Studios, was built by Alvin Lee of the band Ten Years After when he first bought the house. Many recordings were made during Alvin Lee's tenure before he sold the house and studio to David Gilmour of the band Pink Floyd, who used the studio to record parts of the band's 1983 album The Final Cut. Gilmour sold the house and studio to Trevor Horn, formerly of the Buggles, who turned it into Sarm West, a leading recording studio used to record albums by artists such as the Kaiser Chiefs, Charlotte Church and Morrissey. Morrissey referred to Hook End Manor as his spiritual home in his recent autobiography, which is quite a compliment coming from him. There was an unfortunate accident in 2006 when Trevor's wife Jill was accidently shot with an air rifle by their son and remained in a coma until her death several years later. Unfortunately the house, above left, now appears to be vacant.

A memorial to singer Dusty Springfield is in St Mary's churchyard. She was cremated and some of her ashes were buried at the memorial, while the rest were scattered by her brother, Tom Springfield, at the Cliffs of Moher, County Clare, Ireland. The gravestone remains a point of pilgrimage for many fans.

Other popular musicians still living in the areas include:
- Ian Paice, bassist for Deep Purple lives at Shiplake. Deep Purple is another band that recorded at Hook End. Keyboardist Jon Lord lived at Fawley until his death in 2012.
- George Michael has a house in Goring.
- Liam Gallagher of Oasis has a second home at Henley.
- Joe Brown and his daughter Sam – who leads a local Ukulele band.
- Singer Vince Hill lives in Shiplake.

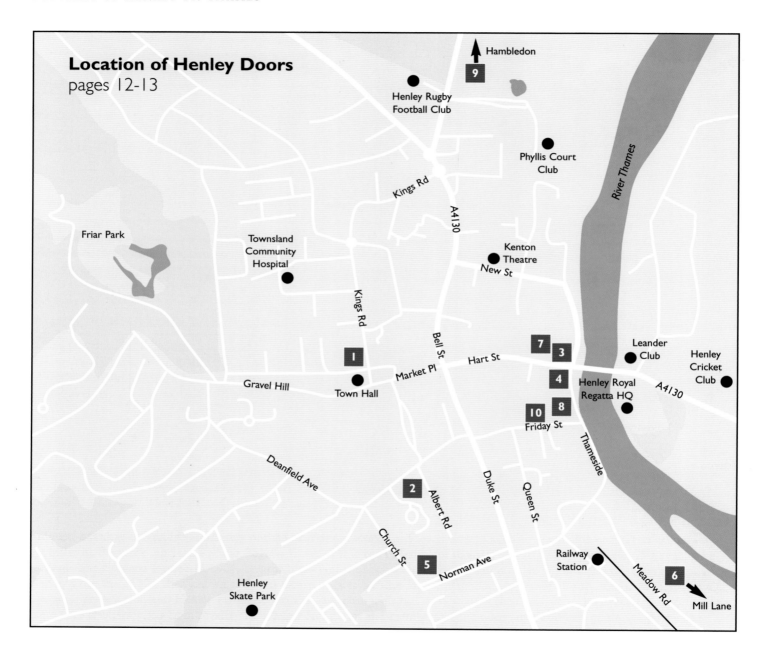

Location of Henley Doors
pages 12-13

Hambledon
9

Henley Rugby
Football Club

Phyllis Court
Club

River Thames

Kings Rd

A4130

Friar Park

Townsland
Community
Hospital

Kenton
Theatre

New St

Kings Rd

Bell St

7   3

Leander
Club

Henley
Cricket
Club

1

Hart St

Gravel Hill

Market Pl

4

Town Hall

Henley Royal
Regatta HQ

A4130

10   8

Friday St

Thameside

Deanfield Ave

2

Albert Rd

Duke St

Queen St

Church St

5   Norman Ave

Railway
Station

Meadow Rd

6

Mill Lane

Henley
Skate Park

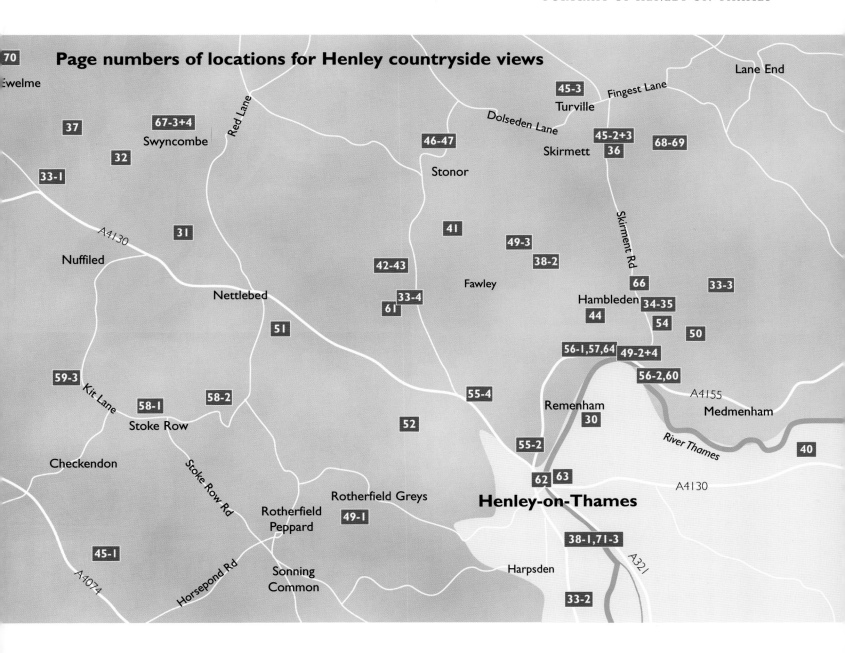

Page numbers of locations for Henley countryside views

70
Ewelme

37

67-3+4
Swyncombe

32

33-1

A4130

31

Nuffiled

Red Lane

Nettlebed

51

59-3

Kit Lane

58-1

58-2

Stoke Row

Checkendon

Stoke Row Rd

45-1

A4074

Horsepond Rd

Rotherfield Peppard

Sonning Common

Rotherfield Greys

49-1

52

46-47

Stonor

41

42-43

33-4
61

Fawley

49-3

38-2

55-4

45-3
Turville

Dolseden Lane

Fingest Lane

Lane End

45-2+3
36
Skirmett

68-69

Skirment Rd

66

Hambleden
44

34-35

54

33-3

50

56-1,57,64   49-2+4

56-2,60

A4155

Remenham
30

Medmenham

55-2

River Thames

40

62 63

Henley-on-Thames

A4130

A321

38-1,71-3

Harpsden

33-2

143

Photo by Scarlet Page

Originally from the US, Jim Donahue has lived in the UK since 1997. He is winner of 2015's British Lifestyle Photography Award for rural photography. He developed his unique formula for capturing the beauty of British countryside combined with community life in previous books on Pangbourne and Whitchurch on Thames, and now uses it to convey the beauty of Henley with fresh eyes. His appreciation for British community life comes partly from his work as a parish councillor and leader of a local sustainability group. His son, William, asked him to include photos of their cats Sammy and Oscar, above.

"Growing up in America and moving to the UK as an adult, I feel that I have an even greater appreciation of the beauty of the area and strong community spirit that is unique to the UK. My passion for photography is driven by the challenge of conveying how beautiful the South Oxfordshire Chilterns are and the community life of its villages, with Henley being the ultimate challenge."

You can see more of Jim's photos on:
http://jimdonahueimages.photoshelter.com/